Lincolnshire
COUNTY COUNCIL

COMMUNITIES, CULTURAL SERVICES
and ADULT EDUCATION

**This book should be returned on or before
the last date shown below.**

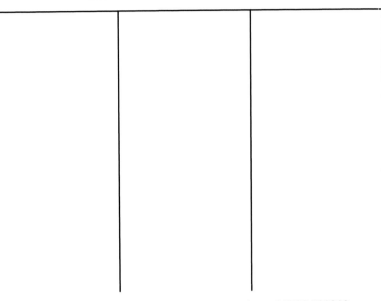

To renew or order library books please telephone 01522 782010
or visit www.lincolnshire.gov.uk
You will require a Personal Identification Number.
Ask any member of staff for this.

EC. 199 (LIBS): RS/L5/19

D0307004

Living in the

1930s

Rosemary Rees & Judith Maguire

Heinemann Library,
an imprint of Heinemann Publishers (Oxford) Ltd,
Halley Court, Jordan Hill, Oxford, OX2 8EJ

OXFORD LONDON EDINBURGH
MADRID PARIS ATHENS BOLOGNA
MELBOURNE SYDNEY AUCKLAND
SINGAPORE TOKYO IBADAN
NAIROBI GABORONE HARARE
PORTSMOUTH NH (USA)

First published 1993
93 94 95 96 10 9 8 7 6 5 4 3 2 1

British Library Cataloguing in Publication Data
is available on request from the British Library.

ISBN 0 431 07219 1

Designed by Philip Parkhouse
Printed and bound in China

Acknowledgements
The authors and publisher would like to thank the following
for permission to reproduce photographs:
Advertising Archive: p. 21
Hulton Picture Company: pp. 7, 8, 12, 13, 15, 16, 17, 23, 26, 28, 29
Robert Opie Collection: p. 18
Philip Parkhouse: p. 4
Popperfoto: pp. 6, 19, 20, 25, 27
Con Dawson: pp. 22, 24, 30
Topham: pp. 4, 5, 9, 10, 11, 14

Cover photograph: Hulton Picture Company

Contents

Home 1

This house was built in the 1930s.
Some young people bought houses like this when they got married.
In the 1930s, this house cost about £500.
Lots of houses like this were built.

In the 1930s, people did not have electric washing machines.
Clothes were washed by hand in a bowl.
Sheets were washed in a dolly tub.
This picture shows a dolly tub and two instruments used for beating the clothes.

Home 2

In the 1930s, lots of women read magazines like the one in the picture. The magazines told women about the best ways to look after their families and their homes.

There were stories to read and recipes to cook.

This is an advert for a vacuum cleaner that was made in the 1930s.
Does it look like the one you have at home?
Vacuum cleaners were very expensive to buy. Many people used brushes to clean their homes.

Home 3

In the 1930s, there were no supermarkets. Everybody went to a butcher to buy meat. When they had chosen the meat they wanted, the butcher's boy would take it home for them on his bicycle.

The shop assistant had to fetch
everything the customer wanted and
bring it to the counter.
There were no electric tills or
calculators in the 1930s.
The shop assistant had to add up what
everything cost.
Shopping took a long time.

School 1

Children enjoyed playing in their school playground.
Sometimes children played with hoops.
The hoops were made from wood.
They made their hoops roll along by hitting them with a stick.
What do you play at playtime?

This is a picture of children in their classroom in the 1930s.
All the desks faced the same way and were often screwed to the floor.
The children were not allowed to move about in the classroom, and they were not allowed to talk.
How is your classroom different?

School 2

Older girls in school had to learn about looking after a home.

In this picture they are learning how to wash clothes.

They used a tin bowl and a big bar of soap.

The soap made their hands very sore.

At school, children could buy a little
bottle of milk each day.
In 1934, each bottle cost about 1p.
In 1939, the school milk was free.
School children drank about 16 million
pints of milk every month.

School 3

These girls had P.E. lessons in their school gym.
They learned to climb up ropes and ladders. They learned to jump and balance on the apparatus in the gym.
What are the girls wearing in this picture? What do you wear for P.E?
Does your P.E. kit look like this?

These boys played rugby at school.
After school, they enjoyed going to their
local playground.
They played football and other games
there.

Work 1

In the 1930s, many people had no work.
They became poor and hungry.
This picture shows some men from a town
called Jarrow.
These men marched 450 miles to
London, to show people that they
wanted jobs.
People gave them food on the way.

In the 1930s, farm work was done by
hand. There was very little
machinery.
Horses were used to plough the fields.
The plough turned the soil over and made
it ready to plant the seeds.
Do you think that horses can plough a
field faster than a tractor?

Work 2

These men made Morris cars in a factory
in 1930.
The cars moved slowly along in a line.
Each part of the car was added by
different men.
These men have put doors on to the car.
In 1930 a Morris car cost about £200.

In the 1930s, many women worked in offices like this one.

They sat at desks all day typing letters.

There were no electric typewriters in the 1930s.

Men did not do any typing then. Do you think that this has changed?

Spare Time 1

In the 1930s, there were not many parks for children to play in.
Children who lived in towns and cities played in the streets.
In the 1930s, there were not many cars and lorries on the roads.
It was safe to play in the street.
Where do you play?

In the 1930s, no-one had a television at home.
People went to the cinema every week.
All cinemas showed special films for children.
These children are queuing up to see their favourite films. It cost 6d to get in.
That is less than 3p.

Spare Time 2

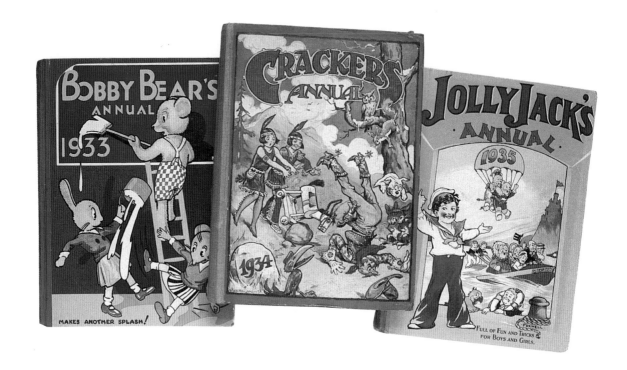

Most children in the 1930s read comics.
These are annuals of some of the comics
they read.
Comics cost about 2d in the 1930s.
That is 1p.
Do you think that your comics are very
different from these comics?

Many people enjoyed dancing in the 1930s.

A band played the music for people to dance to.

They danced waltzes, fox-trots and other dances.

Sometimes the couple who danced the best won a prize.

Holidays 1

In the 1930s, people did not go abroad
for their holiday.

Many people who lived in London went to
Southend for their holiday.

This picture shows a very crowded beach
at Southend.

Look at the clothes people are wearing.

Do they look comfortable?

In the 1930s, cameras did not cost very much. Lots of people bought them.
They took photographs of their families and friends, and the places they visited.
They stuck them in albums.
All these photographs were taken on a seaside holiday.

Holidays 2

On Bank Holidays all the shops, factories and offices closed. Everyone had a holiday. This photograph was taken on a busy Bank Holiday in May 1931.
People were out and about enjoying themselves. Look at the buses and cars. How are they different today?

Not everyone went to the seaside for their holiday.

Some people went to the country.

They would often camp in a field, like the family in this picture.

You can see them stuffing straw into bags to make mattresses and pillows.

Special Days 1

In May 1937, King George VI was crowned.

Thousands of people went to London to cheer as the new king and queen drove by in a golden coach.

All over the country people had street parties.

It was called Coronation Day.

Everybody knew about special days like
the Coronation.

There were other special days that only
family and friends knew about. This
photograph was taken after a family
wedding in July 1937.

Can you find the bride and groom?

Special Days 2

This picture was taken at a funfair in London.

These young people were enjoying themselves on a swing-boat.

They pulled on the ropes to make the swing-boat go higher and higher.

Time Line

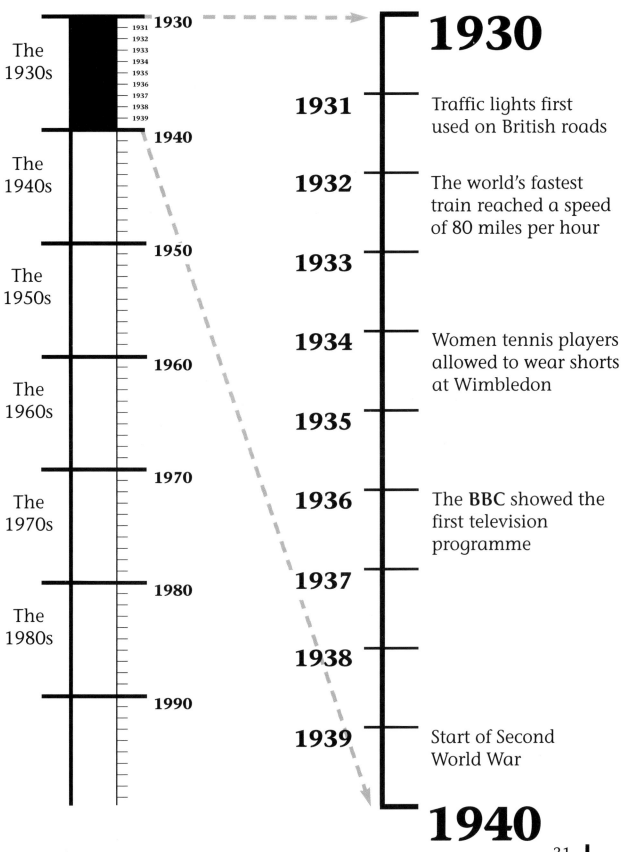

The 1930s

The 1940s

The 1950s

The 1960s

The 1970s

The 1980s

1930
1931
1932
1933
1934
1935
1936
1937
1938
1939
1940

1950

1960

1970

1980

1990

1930

1931 Traffic lights first used on British roads

1932 The world's fastest train reached a speed of 80 miles per hour

1933

1934 Women tennis players allowed to wear shorts at Wimbledon

1935

1936 The **BBC** showed the first television programme

1937

1938

1939 Start of Second World War

1940

Index